LEGACY

To Jacqui
with every
best wish 27/3/18 -

LUCY ANDERSON

L Ac

CinnamonPress

INDEPENDENT INNOVATIVE INTERNATIONAL

Published by Cinnamon Press
Meirion House,
Tanygrisiau
Blaenau Ffestiniog,
Gwynedd, LL41 3SU
www.cinnamonpress.com

The right of Lucy Anderson to be identified as author of this work has been asserted by her in accordance with the Copyright, Designs and Patent Act, 1988. Copyright © 2018 Lucy Anderson.
ISBN: 978-1-910836-97-2

British Library Cataloguing in Publication Data. A CIP record for this book can be obtained from the British Library.

Designed and typeset in Palatino by Cinnamon Press.
Cover design by Jan Fortune.

Printed in Poland

Cinnamon Press is represented in the UK by Inpress Ltd and in Wales by the Welsh Books Council

Contents

Origins:

Embodiment:

Closing:

Thanks to all those who provided the right scent marks.

Origins

Legacy

She places plates
on the tea table:
a slice of meat,
slice of buttered bread,
one tomato each,
quartered, vibrant red.

Her celebration withers in the air,
only the gas lamps hiss,
stilted cutlery on china,
two hearts beating
out of tune,

unable to find each other
across the room choked
with mislaid intimacies.

She smells tomatoes,
thinks of the queue on the market square,
he smells death,
tastes another world.

Father Moth

From dark oak forest
you followed his procession,
single file,

at night, left white silk nest,
fed—not on beach or birch—
but, drink, the streets,

crawled your return,
pulled down wardrobes,
bare-handed—
shredded mothers dresses.

I jumped your back;
small fists into flesh,
your urticating bristles.

On the Singer machine,
Mother sewed me wings;
spanned white, tan, brown,
unable to tell myself from bark.

The Origins of the Big Black Ball

As Big Ben strikes news at ten,
she sits on the stairs,

neither up nor down.

Above, the purple room.
Below, behind the door,

mothers in the front room—
her time, closed time.

Neither up nor down,

the girl, suspended—
can only split herself in two—

give birth to a black ball
she has to hold tight—

no bouncing,
no noise, no fuss.

Drought

that hottest summer,
seven-spotted ladybirds,
heaths to scrubland,
Don, Sheaf, Shirebrook—
cracked gullets,
difficult breaths,

dads sister from America—
nothing to drink—

cousins, country bends,
chicken in baskets,
fourteen days
of standpipes,
limbs fluid to corners of rooms,
until the wet months came.

Slideshow

At the bungalow —
mother, daughter,
unwrap possessions,
dishes clash on cups,
pulses quicken.

At night, pipes creak,
wind and sleet
beat waves on windows.

And he comes —
husband, father.
Tubular doorbell taunts
echo in the hallway,
off key.

They clutch,
mother daughter.
The clocks pendulum swings
from a baby's cries —
to rabid threats.
There is blood, there is blood, he rants.
Head thuds against porch glass.
The girl retches air into air.

The Myth of a Superstar

I knew Abba, the Osmonds,
the edges of Johnny Cash
but not that grandfather
had trained troops,
walked home drunk,
29 miles along railway tracks.

He had a thing for Nana Mouskouri,
a marching cane,
his own language—
nincompoop, old sow,
big girls blouse,
gambled at horses, rummy, cribbage,
chewed on matchsticks,
burnt his legs on the gas,
bragged of missing fingers.

I knew jam, marmite,
golden syrup.
He ate molasses.
His hair jet, greased back,
belly massive, hard
from the medicinal waters
of the Liffey—
                    Guinness on draught.

He covered himself in oil,
fried in the sun,
wore his shirt open low,
rode a moped to our house—
faded red, pushed
                    up   the
                              road.

Unhappy Hour

At dusk, my father
switches from factory to garden,

self-programmed, set to full speed
to clip every rogue sprig
find every leaf,
sweep and sweep,
keep nature tamed
in boundaries.

He labours,
pain-faced, body bent,
demons drown out the call for *Dinner*—
holding this broom as tightly
as he held the bottle.

Incunabulum

The girl serves me
with her Barista machine,
pressures, rolls and steams,
plunges milk wand,
taps pitcher against counter,
circulates and swirls her Latte Art—
foamed milk; small-celled,

says, because it is morning,
she will serve my coffee
in a special mug,
her words—naked skin on skin—

in shifts, nurses once reached in
ungloved hands through portholes
taking the spigot from nose-tube—
its syringe dripping milk two-hourly.
Weak lunged, my alveoli
could not exchange gas,

once a week, my mother
waited at bus stops,
a twenty-mile trip
to see her baby
through glass.

Noost

And what if the midwife had spoken
a different language—a Shetland tongue
to my mother,
when I weighed as a bag of sugar
in my fathers butcher-hands.

What if she had said
this baby girl,
though carved and curved, is softwood,
don't let the bilge water fill her,
keep her moored on dry land.

Noost—a Shetland small boat that is moored on land.

Embodiment

Portrait of Bianca

They have framed me;
big boned,
hair scraped back,
forehead-bare.

You look at me,
I don't quite look at you,

my eyes glazed over,
one half-present, the other past—
the burial of a girl,
in another world.

Tidal

The flood: she rises,
surfs head waves,
takes yellow boat rides
where blue birds bob
and bold ideas
sit on bright horizons.

She laps against rocks,
tricks the ebb,
until her ghost-self

floats grey seas,
with wind-blown waste,
where dead birds flop,
debris gathers,
her bilge waters rise:
the flood.

Ghost Self

Wings fade—orange, yellow,
pale-warning.

She returns, underground,
trails in stars, feeds on milkweed,

clings to dark;
blanket of pins,

each time
a mini-death.

Little Little Girl

after no.24 Susie Mendelesson

She perches, displayed—
nose tilted, toes pointed,
hands swollen to be held.
Finger-nails—knives
to cut herself.

A black curtain hangs,
closed. Little little girl
has crept from underneath,
Into a tiny ring of light, where

she looks to her older self,
turned away—
the delicate cage of her dress
encircling grown up legs and sex.

Figure with Raised Arm

After Georg Bazelitz

In class, the boy puts up his hand
to ask *What am I?*

In the bank, father strides upwards.
In M&S, mother bumps into Marjorie,
a tiny cough at Christopher's name.

Christopher looks at the others,
knows he is not the same.

Alpha-female

Shut away in the dark,
searching eyes know cold,
the barren land.

Spurned—
she snorts,
sprouts male horns,
inflates skin pouch,
amplifies her roar
ready to rut.

With coat of stiff hair,
hooves deeply cleft,
she is firm on marshes,
swift on a diet of forbs,
wild grass.

And she can fight—

fork-headed,
powerful as Dis Pater,
she wins her harem,
sends souls of the dying
to the underworld.

The Outsider

She walks towards me in the road;
Upright, even-paced, my guest,

unaware of the coffin she bears
full of loves I bought, re-bought,

that hanged me, left me ravaged.
My guest, the pall-bearer of love.

Beneath her coat, layers of fine wool,
each one undone, as day unfolds,

but the rooks circle, caw
that my bones have gone to the bone-house.

In the half-light of the graveyard shift,
I stand guard.

A string on my wrist tugs—
the toll of the bell—pall-bearer's kiss.

Corvus frugilegus

You strut,
that winter-
bright spot,
peak-crowned,
red-lilac gloss,

in cast-back light
study your rival,
caw— hoarse.
Blood on glass.

I sacrifice vertebrae,
your low-flight
brings rain.

Working Class Gargoyle

Through rough-cut throat he channels waters,
protects God's house.
His own words choke his gullet.

No smiles or laughter through bored holes,
naso-labial folds, grooves or ruts.
Ugly as sin he faces it out,
teaches perfection with imperfection,
to know the cold, the shadows,

while inside, the privileged
sleep under slabs of alabaster.

Surrounded by sacred soil—black loam,
sand, silt, where scarce plants grow—
river horse tail, wayfaring tree, downy-stalked dog rose,
friars crown—he keeps watch,
their tenderness beyond him.

Daily he toils, daily he weathers
until ground down,
he smoothes,
turns in on himself to feel,
erodes.

Matthew

I

He wakes to God's clock, six a.m., opens his eyes but does not allow them to the light until he has met his breath—the cool of it passing through and out; slow, even, his pace is set.

He turns on his side, raises knees to chest, lifts himself from the bed, places feet upon rushes, scratching on bare soles, welcomed.

The day hints in the small window and with quiet voice he praises God. He tightens his shift at neck, bows head into habit, lets the heavy black cloth unravel and drop about his body, ties himself tight at the waist. And with quiet voice gives thanks to God.

He knows the eight paces to the rere-dorter; how each foot gently rocks in sandals—back and forth, how each foot tilts and falls—side to side beneath the straps.

The feel of buttocks; bony on the plank—damp under the arch where no light is needed, only draught from the hollow below, drawing, with ease, an evacuation of waste, thinking purity to serve God.

In the lavatorium, water waiting to be warmed in the stone lavor with fresh hay and herbs—cleansed for Lauds at the break of day, where he takes his place on the warm wood bench and in voice and body venerates God.

II

He contemplates, as he sits on the cloister stone in afternoon sun and with quiet voice gives thanks to God. Words from Lauds return on his lips, softly escape 'O God, you are my God, I seek you.'

Day surrounds him. The sun's heat penetrates layer by layer—strips him of heavy black cloth, carefully unties and deftly takes off his linen shift and lays him bare. 'My soul thirsts for you; my flesh faints for you.'

Gentle in sandals, he parts his feet, feels his weight. The cool of his breath passes through, leaves as he slips into light, like air. 'O Lord, my lips and my mouth will declare your praise.'

'Praise the Lord! Praise the Lord!' exclaimed, raised higher and higher in steadfast love, soaring God's glory. 'Praise him with trumpet sound, with lute and harp! Praise him with tambourine and dance.'

Yet still he sits, his feet gentle in sandals, placed firm on stone ground under the cloister light. He feels God's power but must not expect its return nor desire it for himself.

In service to God, he knows that tomorrow he will wake to God's clock, open his eyes but not allow them to the light until he has met his breath —the cool of it passing through and out; slow, even, his pace will be set. And with quiet voice he will give thanks to God.

Closing

Stasis

In the church on the hill
of The Fern Green Pasture,
there is a standing still.
No whisper of Kathisma,
her usual flow of bodily liquid stops.
Past, present, future obscure,
tension suspends,
disturbance rubs itself out.
Motionless,
In stasis, like death.

In The Room,

a lavender candle
burns the hours.

Above, the light-shade hangs;
modern, brown suede.

She stores up silence,
announces 'I hate that',

with a hint of finger
pointed from a bone-thin hand.

Beneath, artificial air
pumps the mechanical bed.

Through paper lips
she labours slender breath

pronounces 'Why' or 'Where',
sucks on a baby's cup.

Time Moves

The bells rang a new time.
The mourners stopped,
watched her,
slowed her,
fresh, on the cooling board.
Her eyes were not fading.

They lowered her into the ground—
the coffin—its narrow planks of elm,
wood knots to swell,
resist in the wet,
keep her dry in rosemary, sawdust.
Wrapped in white, she was not darkening.

They put in place the iron cage,
secured her grave,
'a safe for the dead'
to protect her body
from body snatchers
and all the years ahead.
And she was not decaying.

*

Beneath the Taxus Baccata,
Its boughs hollow with age,
she lies, skeletal-dry, bleach-boned,
long cracked in her rusted cage.

Hemimetaboly

Water and tissue,
you return to grass.
I shuffle clippings,
cut them,
multiple times,

set temperature,
weight, sun, shade.

Ounce

Above the treeline,
lineage of Felidae
circle territory.

Crepuscular, stocky,
paws balance weight,
know misstep is disaster.

Hushed chuffles, mews, hisses,
stilled tongue-bones,
breathy snorts.

I sleep under ash-brown sides,
Soft, thick tail
blankets face,

track scent marks;
buttered mash, bean pods,
honeysuckle pomander.

Time Eternal

We, in our keystone
of pale clay,
scratch a time into time.

Our Gnomon may not point exactly
to the North Star,
nor be exactly parallel
to the axis of the earth:

but crudely,
we live moments,
months, live seasons
and turn,
cast shadows,

while time stretches,
without end.

Lightning Source UK Ltd.
Milton Keynes UK
UKOW01f0648060218
317431UK00001B/87/P